Th

Jesus

Story

Told through 25 readings

from the Bible

Lucy Moore

Messy Church® is a registered word mark and the logo is a registered device mark of The Bible Reading Fellowship

Text copyright © Lucy Moore 2014
The author asserts the moral right
to be identified as the author of this work

Published by
The Bible Reading Fellowship
15 The Chambers, Vineyard
Abingdon, OX14 3FE
United Kingdom
Tel: +44 (0)1865 319700
Email: enquiries@brf.org.uk
Website: www.brf.org.uk
BRF is a Registered Charity

ISBN 978 1 84101 583 5
First published 2014
Reprinted 2014
10 9 8 7 6 5 4 3 2 1

Acknowledgements
Scripture quotations marked CEV are taken from the Contemporary English Version of the Bible, published by HarperCollins Publishers, copyright © 1991, 1992, 1995 American Bible Society.

Cover photographs: Cover: red crayon © Photos.com, a division of Getty Images. All rights reserved. Paint splats at bottom: © www.3drenderedlogos.com/Shutterstock.com

Every effort has been made to trace and contact copyright owners for material used in this resource. We apologise for any inadvertent omissions or errors, and would ask those concerned to contact us so that full acknowledgement can be made in the future.

A catalogue record for this book is available from the British Library

Printed in the UK by Zenith Media

Getting stuck into the Bible, not stuck with it.

A lot of people get stuck with the Bible because they treat it like a normal book and start at the beginning. This is logical, but not the best way into such a complicated library of books. There are 66 separate books in the Bible. The first 39 cover the story of the Jewish people up to about 400 years before Jesus' birth, and the final 27 are about Jesus and what happened next.

This little booklet looks at the story of Jesus' life over 2000 years ago in 25 sections. It may be ancient history, but it's surprising how much it tells us about who this unique man is and about who we are ourselves. The stories are taken from the four books about Jesus by Matthew, Mark, Luke and John, called the Gospels. (This just means 'good news'.) We've picked out significant stories about Jesus that between them tell the story of where he came from, what sort of person he was, how he lived, what other people thought of him, what he said about himself, how he died and what the four writers report happening next.

Can you trust the Bible? Is the Jesus story a fairy story or religious advertising? Those are big questions for historians to write about and for you to decide on for yourself from the evidence.

Do Christians claim the Gospels were dropped from heaven? No, and they never have. These books were written by four human beings with God's help, or 'inspired by God', but definitely written by them.

Did the writers make it all up? Almost certainly not: when their books were being read in the early days, there were still plenty of people alive who could have told everyone, 'I met Jesus and he didn't do that!', but there's no historical evidence that anyone claimed they were lies. Other, non-Christian, historians refer to Jesus and to the early Christians, so, yes, he and they most probably existed.

Were the 'Big Four' writing the truth about Jesus as they understood it? Yes, they were. Luke, for example, in his first chapter, explains how much research he had to do to get to the truth from eyewitnesses.

Are the writers impartial observers? No, not at all. They all write as people who are convinced about who Jesus is, and they openly say they want to convince others.

Can you trust them when some parts of what they write contradict other parts? The accounts of Jesus' rising from the dead, for example, are different in details: this might mean one of the writers has got it wrong, or it might be very honest and be a sign that nobody over the years has tried to make them all look consistent by changing the original accounts. They may be different in the same way that eyewitnesses to a road traffic incident can report different details, even if they all agree there was an incident.

We've had to shorten some passages because of space restrictions. The three dots … show where words have been left out, but you can always go and look the passages up in a Bible or online to see them in full. The Bible Gateway website www.biblegateway.com is very easy to find your way around.

On each page you'll find the passage, the book it comes from with chapter and verses, and a comment on why I think it's important or an explanation of what's going on in it.

You might want to read one of these pages every day for a month to give yourself time to think about each one properly. Or you might read it all in one sitting to get the broad sweep. You might read it on your own or together as a family, and talk about it. The booklet will fit in your bag or pocket, so it can go with you to the place where you have time to read it—on the bus or train or in the café, playground or lunch break. Scribble on it; wave it at your local minister or Christian friend and make them answer your questions or listen to your theories. Enjoy it!

OK, here's some background information that helps make sense of something written so long ago and so far away. It's worth remembering that the world was a very different place from the one we live in now. People's attitudes and expectations were not the same as they are today. It was a much crueller place: on the way into the capital city you would regularly walk past the bodies of executed criminals hanging on wooden crosses. It was also much more of a community place: whole villages would go on trips together; extended families would look after each other; and there were very strict written and unwritten rules, especially for women's behaviour. Attitudes to authority were different. Life was slower. It was probably very smelly too.

If you were Jewish around 2000 years ago, you would know the history of what God had done over the years with your nation. It would be recorded in the scrolls of what some now know as the Old Testament (those first 37 books of the Bible)—a collection of stories, laws, history, prayers, prophecies, tragedy and comedy: God at work with his 'chosen people'. (Remember Abraham, Noah, Moses, Joseph, David, Jonah and the big fish…?) All through these scriptures, you would see promises that one day God would send his people a rescuer, a Messiah, a unique person who would be the best king ever, the best high priest ever, the perfect superhero who would set them free for good.

But, by the time Jesus has been born, God seems to have been silent for a very long time—400 years or so! You still continue to worship him and retell the history of what he did in the past, but the ruthless Roman army has invaded your country and has been occupying it for 40 years. There's a Roman governor and Roman soldiers on the street corners, and you have to pay taxes to Rome. You're feeling more oppressed than ever.

In a quiet country corner of this troubled and violent world a young Jewish girl, like the rest of her people, thinks life will be pretty much the same tomorrow as it was yesterday. But God is on the move.

The angel greeted Mary and said, 'You are truly blessed! The Lord is with you.'

Mary was confused by the angel's words and wondered what they meant. Then the angel told Mary, 'Don't be afraid! God is pleased with you, and you will have a son. His name will be Jesus...'

Mary asked the angel, 'How can this happen? I am not married!'

The angel answered, 'The Holy Spirit will come down to you, and God's power will come over you... Nothing is impossible for God!'

Mary said, 'I am the Lord's servant! Let it happen as you have said.'

Luke 1:26–38

The most amazing story ever recorded begins in a village at the back of beyond with an ordinary girl from an unimportant family. Mary is probably about 14 years old when the angel comes with a message for her. If you have a problem with wings and tinsel haloes, as I do, put in the word 'messenger' for 'angel' and see how that feels—in the Bible, angels are simply messengers from God, and we don't actually know what they looked like.

The point is that God chooses to work with ordinary people, like Mary, like Joseph, like you and me. He wants to do incredible things with your life, take you on adventures you'd never dreamed of, give you challenges you'd never asked for! And all he asks is that, like Mary, we say, 'Yes.' Just when Mary thought life would be no more than the fields around the village with an occasional trip up to the big city of Jerusalem as a special treat, her 'yes' changes her whole life from something ordinary into something extraordinary. Because nothing is impossible for God.

What a mess?

About that time Emperor Augustus gave orders for the names of all the people to be listed in record books... Everyone had to go to their own hometown to be listed. So Joseph had to leave Nazareth in Galilee and go to Bethlehem in Judea... Mary was engaged to Joseph and travelled with him to Bethlehem. She was soon going to have a baby, and while they were there, she gave birth to her firstborn son. She dressed him in baby clothes and laid him on a bed of hay, because there was no room for them in the inn.

Luke 2:1–7

The Romans loved everything to be neat, tidy and listed. For Mary and Joseph, the situation is anything but tidy. Imagine the embarrassment when your nosy relatives are whispering, 'Whose baby is it anyway?' and are judging you without knowing the facts. Imagine coping with a birth 80 miles from home. Imagine feeling that you couldn't even provide your own baby with a proper room to be born in or a bed to sleep in. Imagine trying to keep a baby quiet when the house is packed with people.

What does it say about God that he chooses to let Jesus be born into this mess? What might he be trying to say to us in our messy lives about how deeply he understands what we're going through? Or about how important it is to take a moment to consider what really matters in life when everything seems a mess? What would you think of Mary if she whinged about the smell and grumbled about the lack of room service when the Son of God was lying in her arms?

That night in the fields near Bethlehem some shepherds were guarding their sheep. All at once an angel came down to them from the Lord... The shepherds were frightened. But the angel said, 'Don't be afraid! I have good news for you... This very day in King David's hometown a Saviour was born for you. He is Christ the Lord...'

The shepherds said to each other, 'Let's go to Bethlehem and see what the Lord has told us about.' They hurried off and found Mary and Joseph, and they saw the baby lying on a bed of hay.

Luke 2:8–20

When you cut through the fluffy side of this part of the story (pretty angels, 'Come, they told me, pa ra pa pum pum' and so on), it's actually amazing. God could have announced the news of Jesus' birth to anyone, but he chose the people group who were the lowest of the low. Shepherds were pretty grotty: they didn't have baths; they couldn't leave the sheep to go to the synagogue (Jewish 'church') to worship God on the right day; they were pretty much the dregs of society. God chooses to send his messengers to them. This is a breakthrough in religion. There isn't a dividing line any more between the people who are 'in' with God and those who are 'out'—absolutely anybody is welcome to come close to Jesus as the shepherds did. This might not seem revolutionary to us in a fairly egalitarian Western society, but imagine what it would be like if you could go to church only if you were born into a particular family, had gone to a particular university, had a certain amount of money and knew the right people. Instead, the messy shepherds show us that God is throwing open the doors of heaven to absolutely everyone.

Long journeys

When the men went into the house and saw the child with Mary, his mother, they knelt down and worshipped him. They took out their gifts... and gave them to him. Later they were warned in a dream not to return to Herod, and they went back home by another road...

When Herod found out that the wise men from the east had tricked him, he was very angry. He gave orders for his men to kill all the boys who lived in or near Bethlehem and were two years old and younger.

Matthew 2:1–21

About two years after Jesus was born, Mary and Joseph are still in Bethlehem. In nearby Jerusalem the wise men make a claim about who this child is, declaring that he is born to be the king of the Jews. They know this because they've seen it written in the stars. While the ancient world didn't have scientists in the way we understand scientists, these wise men or magi know so much that people think they have supernatural powers—it's where our word 'magic' comes from. Their religious beliefs and their mathematics and astronomy aren't separate subjects but all part of the same search for truth. They are seriously brainy and have travelled seriously far in search of the truth as they understand it. King Herod can't cope with the threat to his throne. The flip side of Christmas not generally shown on jolly Christmas cards is Herod's pointless wholesale slaughter of the male babies and toddlers in Bethlehem. Jesus and his family escape and become refugees in Egypt, far away from all they love. Right from the start, the life of this holy family is far from cosy or safe.

Educating Jesus

After Passover his parents left, but they did not know that Jesus had stayed on in the city… Three days later they found Jesus sitting in the temple, listening to the teachers and asking them questions. Everyone who heard him was surprised at how much he knew and at the answers he gave…

His mother said, 'Son, why have you done this to us? Your father and I have been very worried, and we have been searching for you!'

Jesus answered, 'Why did you have to look for me? Didn't you know that I would be in my Father's house?'

Luke 2:41–52

It's the yearly trip up to the big city of Jerusalem—the big village outing during which everyone keeps an eye out for everyone else's kids. Jesus, who is now twelve and considered just about grown-up in that society, goes missing, and for three days nobody can find him, however hard his parents search the city. When they do find him, he's not smoking behind the bingo hall or drinking shots in the bar but getting as much extracurricular education as he can from the best teachers around. The teachers are gobsmacked by his answers; his parents can't believe what's going on; Jesus himself is the only chilled one and doesn't seem to understand why they've been so worried. From his point of view, it's obvious where he would be: 'in my Father's house'. The angels said twelve years ago who they thought Jesus was. The wise men said who they thought he was. Now here is Jesus himself, showing who he thinks he is by the way he behaves and by his own words. Is he being arrogant? Insensitive? A typical teenager? Or quietly convinced of who he is and where he belongs?

------- Get rid of the mess -------

John the Baptist appeared in the desert and told everyone, 'Turn back to God and be baptised! Then your sins will be forgiven.' From all Judea and Jerusalem crowds of people went to John. They told how sorry they were for their sins, and he baptised them in the Jordan River.

John wore clothes made of camel's hair. He had a leather strap around his waist and ate grasshoppers and wild honey.

John also told the people, 'Someone more powerful is going to come. And I am not good enough even to stoop down and untie his sandals. I baptise you with water, but he will baptise you with the Holy Spirit!'

Mark 1:1–8

John is Jesus' wild and hippie cousin with a strange taste in bush tucker, born a few months before Jesus. Here we see John getting people ready to meet Jesus. Crowds come to him, driven out to the desert by restlessness, 'There must be more to life than this', and the need to get rid of their guilt somehow. John washes them clean of everything holding them back from being the people God wants them to be. He's like a dishwasher making a plate ready to hold food, or a mechanic getting a car ready to hit the road again. John knows the limits of what he can do on his own. He knows there's more to a full life than just washing away what's holding people back. He knows too that when Jesus comes, he'll be able to do far more than just take away the bad stuff. Jesus has powers in a totally different dimension.

Christians know the need to get ready before they meet with Jesus. That's why many church services include confession prayers—'sorry' prayers—near the start. They're an opportunity to reflect on the rubbish we've picked up in life and to get rid of it, as if it's being washed away in a river.

-----A tough time for a tough man- - -

About that time Jesus came from Nazareth in Galilee, and John baptised him in the River Jordan. As soon as Jesus came out of the water, he saw the sky open and the Holy Spirit coming down to him like a dove. A voice from heaven said, 'You are my own dear Son, and I am pleased with you.' Straight away God's Spirit made Jesus go into the desert. He stayed there for forty days while Satan tested him. Jesus was with the wild animals, but angels took care of him.

Mark 1:9–13

This vivid scene takes place right at the start of Jesus' three years of working for the kingdom of God. Up to now he has been a clever boy, a responsible son and big brother and a chippy with rough hands. His mum's stories of shepherds, angels and wise men were 30 years in the past. Now, as he chooses what direction he will go in life, he needs to be sure what God wants him to be and do. He gets ready by choosing to be one of the crowd and to be baptised like every other human being there, not because he's done anything wrong but because he is fully human, just like us. It's a good choice: God's Spirit comes down on him and God the Father tells him who he is. Father, Son and Holy Spirit, all together.

Straight after this spiritual high, Jesus goes out to the toughest place in the area—the desert. He faces not only hunger, thirst and discomfort but soul-searching and a crisis of identity. Jesus is really human and there is nothing we could possibly face, physical, spiritual or mental, that he hasn't been through already.

Funny fishing

As Jesus was walking along the shore of Lake Galilee, he saw Simon and his brother Andrew. They were fishermen and were casting their nets into the lake. Jesus said to them, 'Come with me! I will teach you how to bring in people instead of fish.' Right then the two brothers dropped their nets and went with him.

Jesus walked on and soon saw James and John, the sons of Zebedee. They were in a boat, mending their nets. At once Jesus asked them to come with him. They left their father in the boat with the hired workers and went with him.

Mark 1:16–20

A teenage friend posted photo after photo of herself at Butlin's® with a member of a pop group she'd been following on Twitter and had finally got to meet in the flesh. She couldn't stop talking about him. If he'd said, 'Leave school and come with me,' no question, she'd have done it!

How do you react if someone says, 'Come with me'? I guess it all depends on who it is and how they say it. If it's someone you already think is the bee's knees, someone you've been talking about incessantly, admiring and wishing you could spend more time with, someone it's an unbelievable honour to be with, you might well drop everything and do just what they said. For these fishermen and for the other people Jesus invites to follow him, his invitation is an unmissable opportunity. This is their chance to be close to someone they admire and respect, someone like no one they've ever met before. It's a chance to go in a completely new direction. They'd be mad to turn it down. But what is it about Jesus that makes them so sure they're doing the right thing? Imagine Jesus saying to you, 'Come with me!' How do you react?

·-----·Loser to winner (via dinner)·--·--·

Jesus was going through Jericho, where a man named Zacchaeus lived. He was in charge of collecting taxes and was very rich... But Zacchaeus was a short man and could not see over the crowd. So he ran ahead and climbed up into a sycamore tree.

When Jesus got there, he looked up and said, 'Zacchaeus, hurry down! I want to stay with you today.' Zacchaeus hurried down and gladly welcomed Jesus...

Later that day Zacchaeus stood up and said to the Lord, 'I will give half of my property to the poor. And I will now pay back four times as much to everyone I have ever cheated.'

Luke 19:1–10

Nobody approves of Jesus' actually going to the house of this scum-of-the-earth little man, this distinctly dodgy geezer. Surely, they mutter, Jesus should hang out with nice people? But Jesus doesn't care what anyone else's agenda is. He has his own. He wants to set people free from what holds them back from living the best life possible. He wants communities to be transformed. That's what the kingdom of heaven is all about. He spots Zacchaeus in the crowd and somehow knows him and sees the potential in him. Jesus knows what's holding Zacchaeus back and knows he has the power to set him free, not by a miracle but simply by going and eating with him. Listening to him. Treating him as a human being.

At the end of the meal not only is Zacchaeus a changed man but his actions transform the community of Jericho as well, as justice is done and people are repaid the money that had been stolen from them. Jesus knows exactly who he is and what he's been put on earth to do, and isn't swayed by anyone else's opinion. His single-minded vision for people and communities has the power to transform lives for the better.

Jesus sees the real you that no one else knows. And he loves you.

[Jesus said,] 'Anyone who hears and obeys these teachings of mine is like a wise person who built a house on solid rock. Rain poured down, rivers flooded, and winds beat against that house. But it did not fall, because it was built on solid rock.

Anyone who hears my teachings and doesn't obey them is like a foolish person who built a house on sand. The rain poured down, the rivers flooded, and the winds blew and beat against that house. Finally, it fell with a crash.'

When Jesus finished speaking, the crowds were surprised at his teaching...

Matthew 7:24–29

Well, they would be surprised, wouldn't they? Usually Jewish teachers would base what they were saying on a wise teacher from the past, and put references and footnotes around their own comments on those wise sayings. Here Jesus is speaking as if he is the one to listen to, the one who doesn't need to refer to any other authority, the one who's as dependable as a rock-solid foundation for your house. My words, he says, are going to stand the test of time, will be reliable even when tough times come to you and will provide a firm standpoint, whatever the changing circumstances of your life. It's a pretty big claim. Is Jesus being arrogant or misguided, or is he just saying it how it is so that we can believe him and get on with the best life possible? On which of his words and actions would you be prepared to base your life? Have you ever tried making a decision based on something Jesus said or did? Watch out for an opportunity to give it a try today.

After Jesus left in a boat with his disciples, a terrible storm suddenly struck the lake, and waves started splashing into their boat.

Jesus was sound asleep, so the disciples went over to him and woke him up. They said, 'Lord, save us! We're going to drown!'

But Jesus replied, 'Why are you so afraid? You don't have much faith.' Then he got up and ordered the wind and the waves to calm down. And everything was calm.

The men in the boat were amazed and said, 'Who is this? Even the wind and the waves obey him.'

Matthew 8:23–27

Jesus keeps his friends on their toes. They never know what's round the next corner. They can't predict how he's going to react. Over and over again, he does the unexpected, turns their worlds upside down, makes them see things in a new way. Jesus isn't a 'nice' person. He doesn't tell his friends what they want to hear. When they're terrified and convinced they are about to die in the storm, he doesn't pat them on the head and offer them counselling. Instead, he seems exasperated and perhaps disappointed by their lack of trust in him. 'Look, Jesus, what did you expect us to do?' they must have wanted to shout back at him. But, before they can gather their wits, he stands up in the middle of the rocking boat and, with a word, takes all the power out of the storm. There's no room for grumpiness after something as unexpected as that—the disciples are left simply amazed. Jesus may not be 'nice', but he has the power to control the forces of nature single-handed. Who on earth is he?

A big picnic

When Jesus saw the large crowd coming toward him, he asked... 'Where will we get enough food to feed all these people?'... Andrew... said, 'There is a boy here who has five ... loaves... and two fish. But what good is that with all these people?'...

Jesus took the bread in his hands and gave thanks to God. Then he passed the bread to the people, and he did the same with the fish, until everyone had plenty to eat. The people ate all they wanted, and Jesus told his disciples to gather up the leftovers, so that nothing would be wasted.

John 6:1–14

Jesus certainly knows what people need. When he sees the crowd coming towards him at the back of beyond, his first thought isn't 'How important am I!'; it's concern for these people who must be so hungry. His disciples once again can't see a way out of the problem and laugh at Jesus' idea of even imagining feeding all those people, especially with one tiny picnic. Jesus again turns their idea of him upside down. He doesn't just have kind thoughts about how hungry these people are. He takes the boy's tiny offering and suddenly, somehow, a whole crowd of 5000 men plus women plus children are all satisfied, content, full up. Jesus shows what sort of a person he is by this over-the-top act of generosity, charging nothing, demanding nothing in return, just pouring out what people need out of the goodness of his heart, because that's his character, the person he is.

When we live in God's story, we start to see how he works.

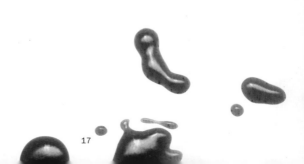

------- Knowing your place -------

The Lord and his disciples were travelling along and... a woman named Martha welcomed him into her home. She had a sister named Mary, who sat down in front of the Lord and was listening to what he said. Martha was worried about all that had to be done. Finally, she went to Jesus and said, 'Lord, doesn't it bother you that my sister has left me to do all the work by myself? Tell her to come and help me!'

The Lord answered, 'Martha, Martha! You are worried and upset about so many things, but only one thing is necessary. Mary has chosen what is best, and it will not be taken away from her.'

Luke 10:38–42

Sharp intake of breath: a mere woman sitting at the feet of a teacher? In those days her place was very definitely in the kitchen, waiting on the men, thank you very much. When Martha tries to make Jesus see how it ought to be, how it always has been, he once again turns things upside down. According to Jesus, Mary has chosen 'what is best'. She puts her friendship with Jesus ahead of tradition and ahead of all the busyness of the jobs that need doing. It would be pleasant to think that the disciples bustled about and finished getting the meal ready while Martha sat down with Jesus too, but perhaps that would have been one revolution too far.

Jesus lived in an ordinary family for 30 years: he knew how much work was involved in the day-to-day running of a household, in welcoming guests to your home. I don't think he was being mean to Martha as she frantically chopped and fried things—that wouldn't fit with his character. Maybe he did want to lift some heavy burdens from her and point her towards what—or rather who—really matters in life.

Martha said to Jesus, 'Lord, if you had been here, my brother would not have died. Yet even now I know that God will do anything you ask.'

Jesus told her, 'Your brother will live again! ... I am the one who raises the dead to life! Everyone who has faith in me will live, even if they die. And everyone who lives because of faith in me will never really die. Do you believe this?'

'Yes, Lord!' she replied. 'I believe that you are Christ, the Son of God. You are the one we hoped would come into the world.'

John 11:21–27

We met Martha and Mary in the last story. Now we read of a tragedy that blows their world apart: their brother Lazarus has died. It seems that Jesus has deliberately not gone to them until it is too late. Mary is so upset she doesn't even come out to greet Jesus when he arrives. Perhaps she blames him for not coming to heal her brother in time. But Martha is now rock solid. 'If you'd been here you would have sorted it...' 'Even now you can make it all OK...' 'Yes, I believe in you even in the face of this disaster.'

When disaster hits us, do we hide away from Jesus, or do we go to him and tell him what we're going through? Do we give him a chance to be with us in our grief? Is our faith the rock-solid sort that nothing, however appalling, can demolish?

Martha's faith gives Jesus the opportunity to make the mind-blowing statement that is still read out at funerals today. He goes on not just to speak but to act, when he calls Lazarus out from his tomb into new life.

'Jesus wept' (v. 35). The shortest verse in the Bible comes in this story. Jesus is with us, not as a distant force but as a friend who knows just how our tragedies feel.

------ -Opening ceremony.------

A large crowd was in Jerusalem for Passover. When they heard that Jesus was coming for the festival, they took palm branches and went out to greet him. They shouted,

'Hooray! God bless the one who comes in the name of the Lord! God bless the King of Israel!'

Jesus found a donkey and rode on it, just as the Scriptures say... Everything had happened exactly as the Scriptures said it would.

A crowd had come to meet Jesus because they had seen him call Lazarus out of the tomb. They kept talking about him and this miracle.

John 12:12–18

Party time in Jerusalem. Jewish people are there from all over the world to remember God's amazing rescue thousands of years ago when he set his people free from slavery in Egypt. Sacrificial lambs are killed by the hundred. Bread is broken. Wine is drunk. It's a time to remember who they are as a people, who their God is and what he's done for them. And Jesus rides into this electric atmosphere with history sparking off around him. He deliberately rides a donkey to make one of the ancient prophecies point to him as God's chosen rescuer—the Messiah. If he wants to annoy the religious leaders, this is an ideal way to do it. If he wants to irritate the Roman occupying forces in this volatile city, it's a good start.

We know the end of the story, but the people in the crowds on this day know only that here is someone who might be the one with the power to set them free, the hero they've been waiting for. Yet they see him only as their rescuer from the Romans, not as their rescuer from the occupying power of death. They still don't know how powerful Jesus really is.

Jesus … went into the temple and began chasing out everyone who was selling and buying. He turned over the tables of the moneychangers and the benches… Jesus would not let anyone carry things through the temple. Then he … said, 'The Scriptures say, "My house should be called a place of worship for all nations." But you have made it a place where robbers hide!'

The chief priests and the teachers … heard what Jesus said, and they started looking for a way to kill him. They were afraid of him, because the crowds were completely amazed at his teaching.

Mark 11:15–18

If you see someone or something you love being treated like scum, you do something about it. Jesus is passionate about God and God's people. To see God's holy place being used for a jumble sale to make a few people rich at the expense of everyone else makes him furious. He creates havoc, as with his carpenter's muscles he physically clears away the trappings of exploitation and greed. He makes the temple fit for what it was made to be: a space set apart for worship, a symbol of God's presence in the middle of his people.

Imagine that furious strength and passion unleashed in your own life. Imagine that power driving out everything in your heart and in your home or work life that stops you being the person you're made to be.

No wonder the chief priests and teachers are even more determined to shut this man up for good: he disrupts their tidy status quo and pulls apart their power systems. He shows them who they are in God's eyes, and it's too painful for them to deal with.

Shady dealings

At that time the chief priests and the nation's leaders were meeting at the home of Caiaphas the high priest. They secretly planned to have Jesus arrested and put to death. But they said, 'We must not do it during Passover, because the people will riot.' …

Judas Iscariot was one of the twelve disciples. He went to the chief priests and asked, 'How much will you give me if I help you arrest Jesus?' They paid Judas thirty silver coins, and from then on he started looking for a good chance to betray Jesus.

Matthew 26:3–5, 14–16

It's fascinating that no one outside Bond or Disney films calls themselves a villain. People always find a very good reason to justify the actions they're taking. The chief priests may have genuinely seen Jesus as a threat to the Jewish people. Judas may have wanted to bring things to a head and give Jesus a chance to show his amazing power when confronted with his enemies. 'I'm only acting for the good of others,' they might say. Jesus knows exactly what their plotting will bring. Even their dodgy dealings are part of God's plan to do something better than the blinkered priests or poor Judas could ever have dreamed of.

Where the '…' is in the reading above, comes a separate story. A woman pours her priceless perfume over Jesus' head. Her action is silent, simple, spontaneous and sincere. It's a bright contrast to the shady goings-on behind closed doors, as those powerful, righteous men plot and scheme and as Judas slips over to the dark side. She doesn't try to manipulate events; she simply offers what she thinks will give Jesus joy. And it does. 'She has done a beautiful thing for me,' says Jesus.

`- - - - -` A never-ending meal `- - - - -`

Jesus took some bread in his hands and gave thanks for it. He broke the bread and handed it to his apostles. Then he said, 'This is my body, which is given for you. Eat this as a way of remembering me!' After the meal he took another cup of wine in his hands. Then he said, 'This is my blood. It is poured out for you, and with it God makes his new agreement. The one who will betray me is here at the table with me! The Son of Man will die in the way that has been decided for him, but it will be terrible for the one who betrays him!'

Luke 22:19–22

In these few hours before his death, Jesus knew what was in store for him. The Gospel writers make it absolutely clear over and over again that he knew what lay in wait for him. He would have seen crucifixions before and heard the screams. Here he thinks only of the people he's leaving behind. He washes their feet first, deliberately and shockingly being their slave to set an example of how they should treat other people once he's gone. In the bread and wine he gives them a way of remembering him that the cleverest and the most ignorant, the youngest and the oldest can all take part in. He knows how dreadful it's going to be for Judas when he realises what he's done, and he has pity for him. In John's account of this night, Jesus prays a long and beautiful prayer for his friends, asking God to keep them safe. Faced with the toughest ordeal of his life, Jesus puts others first and loves them to the last.

.- - - - -. Get me out of here... .- - - - -.

Jesus went with his disciples to a place called Gethsemane, and he told them, 'Sit here while I pray.' Jesus took along Peter, James and John. He was sad and troubled and told them, 'I am so sad that I feel as if I am dying. Stay here and keep awake with me.'

Jesus walked on a little way. Then he knelt down on the ground and prayed, 'Father, if it is possible, don't let this happen to me! Father, you can do anything. Don't make me suffer by having me drink from this cup. But do what you want, and not what I want.'

Mark 14:32–36

Did Jesus have a death wish? Was life on this earth empty and meaningless to him? This quiet scene in the dark among the olive trees shows us instead a Jesus who loves life passionately, who longs to carry on enjoying this beautiful planet with his family and friends, working, eating, drinking and partying. He sees with terrifying clarity what is coming to him the next day and is beside himself with fear. Jesus is facing the biggest crisis of his life. As in the desert after his baptism, he can choose the easy way or the right way. He begs his loving Father for a way out, but when there isn't one, he knows what he has to do. He's so sure of who he is and what he has come to do that he can still pray, 'Do what you want, and not what I want.'

In the children's novel *The Lion, the Witch and the Wardrobe* by C.S. Lewis, Aslan is glad to have Lucy and Susan close to him before he faces the witch. Here we see Jesus, too, needing his friends around him. Instead of keeping awake with Jesus, they fall asleep. He must have felt so alone.

- - - · When the going gets tough. _ _ ·

Peter sat there with them, and a servant girl saw him. Then after she had looked at him carefully, she said, 'This man was with Jesus!'

Peter said, 'Woman, I don't even know that man!'

A little later someone else saw Peter and said, 'You are one of them!'

'No, I'm not!' Peter replied.

… Another man insisted, 'This man must have been with Jesus…'

Peter replied, 'I don't know what you are talking about!' Right then, while Peter was still speaking, a rooster crowed.

The Lord turned and looked at Peter. And Peter remembered that the Lord had said, 'Before a rooster crows tomorrow morning, you will say three times that you don't know me.' Then Peter went out and cried hard.

Luke 22:54–62

The quiet of the garden is broken as Judas arrives with a crowd. He gives Jesus the usual kiss of greeting, the ironic secret sign to the soldiers that this is the man to grab. From now on, events unravel with increasing violence and emotion. The disciples, who had cheerily promised to stick with Jesus whatever happened, now do a runner to save their own skins. Peter hides in the shadows and follows the soldiers at a safe distance to see what happens to Jesus. He sits in the cold grey predawn light at a fire in the courtyard, waiting for Jesus to be brought out of the building where they'd taken him. People start to peer at him and notice his accent. One after another, they insist he was one of the gang who hung out with that Jesus who's just been arrested. Again and again and again, Peter insists Jesus is nothing to do with him. How has he disintegrated so far, so fast? How has Peter the rock solid turned into this coward who won't even admit he knows his friend? What does Peter see in Jesus' look?

------- . What is truth?. _ _ _ _ _ _ _ _ -.

Pilate ... called Jesus over and asked, 'Are you the king of the Jews?'...
Jesus answered, 'My kingdom doesn't belong to this world...' 'So you are a
king,' Pilate replied.

'You are saying that I am a king,' Jesus told him. 'I was born into this
world to tell about the truth. And everyone who belongs to the truth knows
my voice.' Pilate asked Jesus, 'What is truth?'

Pilate went back out and said, 'I don't find this man guilty of anything!
And since I usually set a prisoner free for you at Passover, would you like for
me to set free the king of the Jews?'

They shouted, 'No, not him! We want Barabbas.' Now Barabbas was a
terrorist.

John 18:33–40

In a court of law, we expect to find truth and justice to protect the innocent and condemn the guilty. Is there any justice or truth in Jesus' trial in
front of the Jewish high priests during the night? Or in the Roman court
here with the politically hypersensitive Pontius Pilate? The sentence is
pronounced by the crowd! It all seems horribly familiar in our society
with our trial by media, when truth is perverted to sell newspapers or
for political ends. I find these parts of the Christian story very painful to
read. Jesus—this person who has not only done nothing wrong but has
lived his life wholly for God and for other people—hands himself over
to a brutality that he could so easily escape at any point. An innocent
man chooses to allow himself to be tortured physically, spiritually and
mentally for 18 hours. He must have been so certain there was no other
option. Jesus, the man who brings love and life, is sentenced to death.
Barabbas, the man who brings terror and death, is set free.

The end

They nailed Jesus to a cross… Jesus said, 'Father, forgive these people! They don't know what they're doing.'

While the crowd stood there watching Jesus, the soldiers gambled for his clothes. The leaders insulted him by saying, 'He saved others. Now he should save himself, if he really is God's chosen Messiah!' The soldiers made fun of Jesus and brought him some wine. They said, 'If you are the king of the Jews, save yourself!'…

Around noon the sky turned dark and stayed that way until the middle of the afternoon. The sun stopped shining, and the curtain in the temple split down the middle. Jesus shouted, 'Father, I put myself in your hands!' Then he died.

Luke 23:33–46

This wasn't a glorious, romantic, heroic death. It was a messed-up body displayed as embarrassingly as possible, surrounded by people calling out tacky one-liners. Yet Jesus maintains his dignity, loving the very people who are laughing at him. He has had a bigger agenda right from the start, and these people shrink to the stature of gnats beside his more-than-human love. Somehow he knows that he is carrying out the one action that will change humanity's entire cosmic position. The planet knows it: the very sky gets dark; even the spiritual powers know it: the temple curtain rips apart. Only the human beings around him fail to understand the significance of what Jesus is doing.

How do you think of Jesus on the cross? Was it a tragic end to a good man's life? Was it an avoidable error of judgement? An attempt at martyrdom? 'One of those things'? A fake? The deepest expression of suffering the world has ever seen? A deliberate decision to take a painful course of action towards a definite outcome? A mystery? The ultimate expression of God's love for human beings?

The angels asked Mary, 'Why are you crying?'

She answered, 'They have taken away my Lord's body! I don't know where they have put him.'

As soon as Mary said this, she turned around and saw Jesus standing there. But she did not know who he was. Jesus asked her, 'Why are you crying? Who are you looking for?'

She thought he was the gardener and said, 'Sir, if you have taken his body away, please tell me, so I can go and get him.'

Then Jesus said to her, 'Mary!'

John 20:11–16

Mary Magdalene, one of Jesus' friends, has gone to the tomb early in the morning to embalm his body. The body has gone. She fetches Peter and John, but they are no help and, after a forensic examination of the tomb, they go away—Peter baffled, John daring to believe the unbelievable.

Mary is left alone. All she could have done for Jesus was to treat his corpse with respect, and now even that has been taken away from her. She sees two people in the tomb: angels, God's messengers. Remember the way those messengers announced Jesus' birth? Here they are again, not in a stable looking at strips of cloth wrapped round a baby but in another unclean place marvelling at strips of cloth wrapped around a missing body. Mary is so beside herself she doesn't even recognise the voice that echoes the angels' words. It's only when the stranger says her name that she realises who he is and starts to hope again. God's pattern is set for good in this story: utter despair, brokenness and death are turned by God's loving power into utter joy, healing and new life. It's a pattern we can trust for our own lives.

·----· In the hands of the evidence.----·

A week later the disciples were together again. This time, Thomas was with them. Jesus came in while the doors were still locked and stood in the middle of the group. He greeted his disciples and said to Thomas, 'Put your finger here and look at my hands! Put your hand into my side. Stop doubting and have faith!'

Thomas replied, 'You are my Lord and my God!'

Jesus said, 'Thomas, do you have faith because you have seen me? The people who have faith in me without seeing me are the ones who are really blessed!'

John 20:26–29

For some reason Thomas wasn't with the other disciples when Jesus appeared to them after his death, so he swears blind he won't believe this unlikely story of Jesus' coming back from the dead unless he sees and touches Jesus for himself. Thomas is often called 'Doubting Thomas', but I prefer to call him 'Honest Thomas'. Thomas knows what he needs in order to believe. He isn't going to go thoughtlessly along with the crowd. *The Emperor's New Clothes* is not for him.

Jesus also knows what Thomas needs. He gives him the evidence he needs to believe the unbelievable. At the same time, Jesus makes it clear how happy people like us will count ourselves when we believe that Jesus came back to life without having to meet him physically. Personally, I would really like to meet Jesus face to face and touch his hand—but I don't need to. Jesus knows just what each of us needs to put our trust in him as honestly as Thomas does.

· - - ~ · The start of the adventure · _ _ - ·

Jesus' eleven disciples went to a mountain in Galilee, where Jesus had told them to meet him. They saw him and worshipped him, but some of them doubted. Jesus came to them and said:
   'I have been given all authority in heaven and on earth! Go to the people of all nations and make them my disciples. Baptise them in the name of the Father, the Son, and the Holy Spirit, and teach them to do everything I have told you. I will be with you always, even until the end of the world.'

Matthew 28:16–20

I'm sure this rather brusque report is only Matthew's summary of a much longer, gentler, more intimate conversation between Jesus and his friends. Jesus gives them a job. They need to get off their backsides and make sure that everyone from every background has the chance and choice to meet this wonderful man for themselves and to have 'life, and have it fully' (John 10:10)—and that isn't just for this life.

Being Jesus' disciple is simply about making the decision to live the way Jesus demonstrates so that he has people working with him to change the world for the better. It's about bringing hope, justice and healing and about taking light into dark places. It's not about rules and regulations. It's about living as his friend and apprentice, getting it wrong much of the time but learning on the job. It's about lifelong learning how to love—to love God, to love unloveable people around us and to love ourselves. It's like a marriage or like going on an expedition with a leader you admire. It might cost you everything you have; it might change you beyond recognition; it will almost certainly bring trouble. It's an adventure.

- - - - - - - Going on with God - - - - - - -

You've read some of the story of Jesus. Perhaps you say, 'So what?' Perhaps you say, 'Some of this makes sense and makes me think,' or perhaps you say, 'I never knew Jesus is like this! This is someone I want to know better, someone I'd like to have as a role model for my own life, someone I can trust.' If you can see the remotest spark of appeal in Jesus, that's the first tiny step towards becoming a modern-day disciple.

It's different for everyone. You'll need to work out what it means for you. It probably won't involve sandals or beards. For some people, it starts simply with a conversation with God and a gradual handing over of things to him as you find out that he makes a difference. For others, it means a dramatic turnaround from desperate situations.

There isn't one single right way to start off being a disciple. Some people like to use a prayer like this:

Jesus, I want to start living life your way. I know this is going to be difficult and will cost a lot at times. Please set me free from the things that hold me back. Please give me your love and power to change what needs changing. I put myself in your hands from now on. I believe and trust in you, one step at a time.

Or you might just tell Jesus in the silence of your heart that you want to live his way with his help. You might go and talk it through with someone who knows you and can explain the next thing you could do. You might do something symbolic that doesn't involve words at all. You might join a baptism or confirmation course at your local church (you don't have to get baptised or confirmed at the end of it if it turns out not to be the right thing). If you've still got lots of questions, you might find it more helpful to go on a course the church runs for people who are just enquiring.

You do need to find other people to help you out, though. This might be a friend, a minister, a group or a church of some sort. You'll need to be as kind about other disciples as you'd like them to be about you. This will be hard, because we all make mistakes all the time, just as Jesus' original disciples did, but it's all part of learning to love.

The following are a few of the tried-and-tested things that have helped people be Jesus' disciples over the years:

- helping other people
- making the place you live or work a better place
- talking and listening to God
- reading the Bible with the help of study notes or in a group
- worshipping God in a church
- taking Communion
- finding out what your gifts are and using them
- talking about faith stuff to other people who don't yet believe in it

There's lots more, but you'll discover it in time.

Packs of this booklet are available. Please contact your local bookshop, go to www.messychurch.org.uk/thejesusstory/ or or call BRF Customer Services on 01865 319700 for further details.

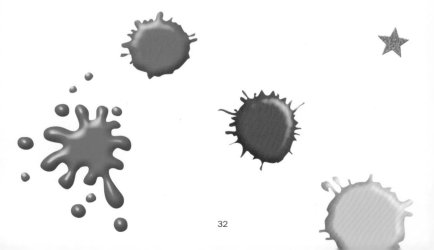